Life in a Victorian Household

First published in the United Kingdom in 2007 by
Sutton Publishing, an imprint of NPI Media Group
Limited · Cirencester Road · Chalford · Stroud ·
Gloucestershire · GL6 8PE

British Library Cataloguing in Publication Data
A catalogue record for this book is available from the
British Library.

ISBN 978-0-7509-4606-3

Typesetting and origination by
NPI Media Group Limited.
Printed and bound in England.

Life In A Victorian Household

PAMELA HORN

SUTTON PUBLISHING

Contents

To my husband,
who has helped in so many different ways.

SHILLINGS AND PENCE CONVERSION TABLE

Old money	Decimal	Old money	Decimal
1d	½p	1s 8d	8½p
2d or 3d	1p	1s 9d or 10d	9p
4d	1½p	1s 11d	9½p
5d	2p	2s	10p
6d	2½p	2s 6d	12½p
1s	5p	3s	15p
1s 1d	5½p	5s	25p
1s 1d or 1s 3d	6p	10s	50p
1s 6d	7½p	20s	100p i.e. £1

CHAPTER 1

Middle-class Victorian Homes

When Seebohm Rowntree conducted his social survey of the people of York in 1899 he took 'the keeping or not keeping of domestic servants... as marking the division between the working classes, and those of a higher social scale'. A large proportion of the maids worked in households with one or two domestics only, around three-fifths of the nation's servant-keepers falling into this category. Among them were artizans and small shopkeepers, like the Bethnal Green woman who employed a ten-year-old girl in the mid-1860's to look after a baby and to serve in the shop. When she was thirteen the girl went to another small London household, where she had a good mistress and plenty of food but had to sleep in a basement kitchen. This swarmed with black-beetles and made her 'very wretched at night'. She also had little free time, being allowed out on Sundays only to go to church. She left after a year.

However, most domestic staff—both male and female—worked in more substantial middle and upper class homes than these, even when they were the sole helper in the house.

The Victorian middle classes have been called 'the most home-centred group in British history'. Charles Dickens in his *Sketches of Young Couples* (1840) claimed that a love of home and the 'English virtues associated with it' provided the 'only true source' of 'domestic felicity'. As society became increasingly industrialized and commercialized, and as growing numbers of the population lived in towns, the home came to be seen as a refuge from the competitive pressures of the wider world. In 1801 around one in five of the 9 million people living in England and Wales were urban dwellers. By 1901, with a total population of 32.5 million, that proportion had swollen to four out of every five residing in towns. Significantly, out of the 32.5 million, around 1.3 million were domestic servants in private households—1.28 million of them women and girls.

Houses came to be seen almost as personal kingdoms, protected from intrusion by those who were not family and friends by the gates, hedges and walls that marked their boundaries. Within this setting, the home served as a focus for entertainment and recreation, as well as for rest and recuperation, particularly for the menfolk when they returned from the daily demands of business or professional life. Outside the house, the gardens of the more affluent became showcases for plants, with carefully cultivated flower beds, and fruit and vegetables grown for the table. Some had hothouses, which enabled more delicate or exotic plants to be raised. Gardens were places for relaxation, too, with afternoon tea served on the lawn, croquet and archery contests organized, and impromptu games played by the children. As the Registrar-General put it, in connection with the 1851 census of population: 'The possession of an entire house is... strongly desired by every Englishman; for it throws a sharp, well-defined circle round his family and hearth—the shrine of his sorrows, joys, and meditations'.

That view was shared by John Ruskin's father, the founder of a prosperous London wine firm, when he declared in sentimental mode: 'Oh! how dull and dreary is the best society I fall into compared with the circle of my own Fire Side with my Love sitting opposite irradiating all around her, and my most extraordinary boy'.

In reality, much of family life did not match this optimistic picture. For many individuals, the intimate daily contacts and close relationships proved stifling and led to quarrels and unhappiness, as John Ruskin's own unfortunate marriage was to demonstrate. Single daughters at home, especially as they grew older, often found the restrictions irksome. In the early l830s, when Florence Nightingale was in her early thirties, she expressed this general discontent, complaining of the role expected of well-to-do women like herself, and the lack of purpose in their lives: 'They are taught from their infancy upwards that it is a wrong, ill-tempered, and a misunderstanding of "woman's mission"... if they do not allow themselves *willingly* to be interrupted at all hours... The actual life is passed in sympathy given and received for a dinner, a party, a piece of furniture, a house built or a garden laid out well, in devotion to your guests... in schemes of schooling for the poor... The time is come when women must do something more than the "domestic hearth".'

Nonetheless, those darker aspects did not prevent society from emphasizing the centrality of family life for the nation's wellbeing. That applied to all classes and in reinforcing the philosophy, religion played its part, through the values and moral standards it imparted and the sense of community which membership of a church or associated religious body engendered. F. M. L. Thompson, in a study of the development of the prosperous London suburb of Hampstead, commented on the high level of Sunday worship recorded in mid-century. He saw this not merely as a manifestation of faith but as an indication of the power of the local church 'to confer social acceptance and assist [the] personal advancement' of those who attended. By that means communities were formed 'out of the individual family atoms' residing on Hampstead's new housing estates.

But the dwellings of prosperous Victorians had another, more public, role alongside the security and privacy they conferred on their occupants. Through their size, appearance, style and location, as well as through the number of domestic workers employed within them, they served as visible symbols of their owner's position in the world. To meet the need for residential 'zoning' linked to this, a multiplicity of suburbs was constructed, each carefully ranked so as to keep the classes apart. Edgbaston, for example, was regarded as the 'Belgravia' of Birmingham, a place where affluent businessmen and professional people lived and where there were prohibitions on the opening of commercial premises within the area. Similarly, Alderley Edge in Cheshire was described in a local guide as the 'residence of the merchant princes of Manchester'. Katharine Chorley, who grew up there at the end of the nineteenth century, claimed that the 'poor people' living in it 'were almost exclusively the personal retainers of the Edge houses, the gardeners, the coachmen and later the chauffeurs'. She then added drily:'Like a large house and garden, a wife or daughter with nothing to do was an emblem of success.There were plenty of servants... so domestic chores were mostly limited to ordering the meals and doing the shopping and domestic responsibility to captaining the staff'. For the rest, they 'filled in time' by paying calls, which was an accepted social duty and, in accordance with the etiquette of the day, was the only means of getting to know new neighbours. 'And it was essential to leave the [calling] cards in correct numbers.To get this wrong showed ignorance of polite manners and therefore brought the caller's whole social position into question'.The younger and more energetic women played golf and tennis, and for the older ladies there was bridge. '"Sewing for charity" filled in a little more time.'

This preoccupation with securing the 'right' address was appreciated by London estate agents, too, when they advertised houses to let to wealthy families coming to the capital to enjoy the pleasures of its social Season, between April or May and July of each year. Care was taken to emphasize that the properties offered were in 'choice' locations or were suitable for 'a family of the highest position', as typical advertisements in *The Times* of 11 and 12 March, 1887, phrased it.

Within the household itself similar concerns about segregation and classification existed, so that those residing 'upstairs' were divided from their domestics, who were 'below stairs'. As Lady Cynthia Asquith commented, it was a time when 'employers and employees ... knew their places, and kept to them as planets to their orbits'. Hence when the architect, Robert Kerr, published his book, *The Gentleman's House* (1864) he selected 'privacy' as the most important feature of such a property. By that he meant the separation of the family from their servants. He put this ahead of other desirable characteristics, such as the comfort of the house and its convenience. To achieve the desired end it was essential that 'Family Rooms [should] be... private, and as much as possible the Family Thoroughfares'.

He considered it the foremost of all maxims, therefore, 'that the Servants' Department shall be separated from the Main House, so that what passes on either side of the boundary shall be both invisible and inaudible on the other'. On the same principle, in large houses, there should be a separate staircase for the sole use of the domestic staff as they went about their duties. Even out of doors it was important that the walks of the family in garden and grounds should 'not be open to view from the Servants' Department.' Whatever the size of the household, 'let the family have free passage without encountering the servants unexpectedly, and let the servants have access to all their duties without coming unexpectedly upon the family or visitors.' The underlying concept was that the 'family [constituted] one community; the servants another.' In such circumstances a system of bell pulls was an essential feature of any well-to-do home, so that the servants could be summoned when needed.

It was part of the same process that what Lady Cynthia Asquith called 'the turmoil, stress, and steamy odorous heat of cooking was kept well battened-down below stairs'. In this way the smells associated with the preparation of food were kept distant from the family's own living quarters. Inevitably this meant dishes had to be carried a considerable distance to the dining room—a practice that meant extra work for the servants and sometimes cold food for the diners.

Even in relatively humble homes, the division between family and servants was often maintained. Flora Thompson noted how in rural Oxfordshire in the 1880s and 1890s while some shopkeepers and tradesmen treated their young maids as 'one of the family' in other households they were 'put into caps and aprons' and had their meals in the kitchen. When, as with one widow, who ran a blacksmith's smithy and acted as village postmistress, the employer herself ate in the kitchen, the maid was provided with a small side-table in the same room for her meals. It indicated her 'separation' from the mistress.

Part of the middle-class desire for their dwellings to be seen as indicators of economic success arose from the long-established example of landed families, for whom the country house had always been more than a home. For grandees at the top of the servant-keeping hierarchy, with retinues of retainers running into dozens, their establishment could constitute 'a settlement as large as a small village'. In this way their house served as a power base, whose imposing structure demonstrated the owner's authority, wealth and superior social status. Its architecture and interior decoration affirmed his cultured taste, education and good breeding, as well as his affluence. As Jessica Gerard has noted, a large country house with its 'opulent hall and reception rooms served as a public stage of the rituals of social performance which presented the family to greatest advantage, enhancing its prestige among social equals and exacting deference from inferiors.'

The middle-class urge to achieve social standing through the size and location of their home was extended to the hospitality they provided and the furnishings and fittings displayed. This led one writer on household management, J. H. Walsh, in his *Manual of Domestic Economy* (1857) to deplore the 'reckless extravagance of expenditure' which occurred when friends and acquaintances vied with one another. 'This is more especially the case in the large provincial towns', he wrote, 'where dinner-parties, evening parties, carriages and horses, expensive clothes and all the various items which help to swell the Christmas bills, are indulged in... Because Mrs. A. has given a large and tastefully-arranged dinner-party, Mrs. B. must out-do her if possible... Every one wishes to be thought a step above his or her real position'. For Walsh, a 'well-ordered English household' was one where 'every real want' was 'quietly and regularly supplied at the cheapest possible rate consistent with good quality'. In choosing the location of a house, the prime concern should be whether it offered good air, good drainage, good soil, and a good water supply rather than other considerations. That was sound advice at a time when typhoid was a major killer and when the death of the Prince Consort in December 1861 was attributed to a contaminated water supply.

The spirit of emulation was extended to house contents, too, despite the criticisms of Walsh and

other authors of household management manuals
who thought like him. Families wanted furniture
and fittings which looked new, stylish and expensive.
Ornaments, mirrors, carpets, curtains, and a
multiplicity of sofas, chairs, tables, and display cabinets,
to say nothing of the all-important pianoforte,
gave many Victorian rooms a cluttered appearance.
In the upper middle-class home of Linley and
Marion Sambourne in Kensington, for example, an
inventory of 1877 revealed that the drawing room,
the centrepiece of the house, contained 250 objects,
including a vast array of ornaments and knick-knacks,
to which they added over the years. To keep these well
dusted must have presented their housemaid with a
formidable task. There were sixty-six upright chairs
in the Sambournes' house, ten of them in the best
bedroom, where they slept. There were two small
tables in that room as well, in addition to the usual
bedroom furniture. The walls were covered with
pictures, including the halls, with sixty-two framed
photographs in the front hall and thirty-five in the
rear hall. Almost three hundred items lined the walls

of the staircase.

It was in this acquisitive and competitive atmosphere that the highly religious Marion Bradley, wife of a master at Rugby school, ruefully noted in her diary during September 1854, that she must economize in her budgeting: 'I cannot see in looking round how I can be more economical in the house, for I always check any extravagance I meet with in the bills... Where I do see my tendency to extravagance is in indulging my taste for elegance in furnishing. I shall not if I can help it spend any more money in adorning rooms nor in uselessly fine dress for the children, but God must be my helper in this resolution... for I am miserably weak.'

Members of the aristocracy greeted with hostility and contempt the ostentation of the aspiring middle classes and, in particular, the attempts at social climbing by the *nouveaux riches*. Lady Frances Balfour, after a visit to Alfred de Rothschild's newly-built Halton House in Buckinghamshire, noted sourly: 'I have seldom seen anything more terribly vulgar... Oh! but the hideousness of everything, the showiness! the sense of lavish wealth thrust up your nose!'

Charles Dickens, too, mocked the pretensions of plutocrats lower down the social scale when he described the 'bran-new house in a bran-new quarter of London' occupied by Mr. and Mrs. Veneering, in his novel, *Our Mutual Friend* (1865):

Everything about the Veneerings was spick and span new. All their furniture was new, all their servants were new, their plate was new... their pictures were new, they themselves were new ... For in the Veneering establishment, from the hall chairs with the new coat of arms, to the grand pianoforte with the new action, and up-stairs again to the new fire-escape, all things were in a state of high varnish and polish. And what was observable in the furniture, was observable in the Veneerings—the surface smelt a little too much of the workshop and was a trifle sticky.

William Morris, the arts and crafts pioneer, in 1879 declared acidly that he had 'never been into any rich man's house which would not have looked the better having a bonfire made outside it of nine-tenths of all that it held.'

Nevertheless, many wives and daughters took pride in newly refurbished rooms and in the admiration their efforts evoked among friends and acquaintances. In late 1889 Jeannette Marshall's parents moved from their old home in Savile Row to a newly-leased property in Cheyne Walk, Chelsea. Their two daughters were given the task of selecting the colour scheme and designs of the new house and they set to with a will. The four drawing-rooms alone had two separate colour schemes and even the servants' bedroom became a matter of pride, with its pale brown paintwork and yellow and white floral paper. On 5 May, 1890, when the family had the first formal 'at home' day for visitors, the girls happily received the plaudits of their guests. Jeannette noted in her diary that those who came had been 'in raptures pure & simple. We had our fill of compliments, & no mistake'. As her biographer puts it, by the move the Marshalls appeared to have 'turned over a new leaf. It was as though acquiring a house worthy of being shown off had bestowed on them the self-assurance and warmth of born hosts'—qualities which had been lacking in their Savile Row days.

Pleasure in home and hospitality was expressed by Marion Sambourne, too. When she returned after even a brief absence she often commented on how attractive everything looked, and 'how glad she was to be back'. She also enjoyed entertaining, as her diary makes clear, 'Delightful dinner here, room looked v. pretty with new lampshades', she noted on one occasion. After another dinner-party she recorded complacently: 'Table looked lovely, yellow green and orange. Arranged flowers & fruits'.

Mrs. Sambourne also enjoyed the hospitality provided by her friends. 'Delightful dinner at Mrs. Powers, delicious food. Magic lantern & music', she wrote on one occasion. Sometimes the music was the most attractive part of the evening. 'To Mrs. Parish's at home, v. slow there. Capital music but heavy company'. She also judged other ladies by the condition of their rooms. In 1894, when visiting a Mrs. Crane, she commented disapprovingly: 'what a dirty house, dust & crumbs of weeks, the wonder is people turn out of such houses looking comparatively clean!' To her, Mrs. Crane was failing in her duty as mistress of her household, something which was seen as a prime female responsibility in Victorian society.

A similar approach of judging a wife by the condition of her house was adopted by Lady Colin Campbell in 1893 when she described the drawing room as 'the lady's room' where 'the character of the lady herself may be told by inspecting that one room!... [E]legant refinement should reign predominant, cheerfulness should go hand in hand with taste.' A high standard of domestic service was also necessary if the establishment were to enjoy a good reputation. 'Neat and tidy servants are essential to the credit of a household', she declared; 'dirty and slovenly attendants stamp it with vulgarity' —and *vulgarity* was a cardinal sin in the best social circles.

CHAPTER 2

Mistress of the Household

It was essential for the well-being of any Victorian family that the household should run smoothly. Mrs. Beeton claimed she had been induced to write her famous *Book of Household Management* (1861) by witnessing the 'discomfort and suffering' brought about by 'household mismanagement. I have always thought that there is no more fruitful source of family discontent than a housewife's badly-cooked dinners and untidy ways'. To avoid this, the mistress must be 'thoroughly acquainted with the theory and practice of cookery, as well as be perfectly conversant with all the other arts of making and keeping a comfortable home.' She should provide leadership to her servants, 'and just in proportion as she performs her duties intelligently and thoroughly, so will her domestics follow in her path.'

The recruitment of competent servants was an important component in achieving that goal, and mistresses needed to recognize this fact. As Mrs. Panton, author of the household management text, *From Kitchen to Garret* (1888), declared firmly: 'Never be afraid to praise your servants, as one lady is I know of, for fear they may think she cannot do without them: we *can't* do without them — why should we pretend we can? They are far more likely to remain where they are appreciated and cared for than where they know they are looked upon as so much necessary furniture.' When deficiencies occurred in the quantity or quality of staff employed, then the whole establishment's reputation suffered. Anne Sturges Bourne, who owned a small country house in Hampshire, had to confess ruefully to a friend in July 1853 that the recent visit of a Miss Hewitt had gone badly. 'I see plainly I must not attempt visitors or children without 3 more servants', for Miss Hewitt had had 'a quick eye for the defects of one's housekeeping'.

In the largest households day-to-day

responsibility for domestic affairs would be taken by the housekeeper and the steward or butler, in consultation with the mistress. 'When I was a child', wrote Lady Cynthia Asquith, 'the lives of all well-to-do families were benevolently ordered by a large staff.' Hence at Englefield House in Berkshire, the housekeeper not only had to 'provide for the Family of 16 to 20 Servants', take care of the household linen, and 'Look after the Rooms when there was company' but she must also keep order 'below stairs' and not allow the maids to go out without her permission: 'take care that they are dressed quietly.'

Occasionally, a well-established housekeeper could present problems for a new mistress. When twenty-one-year-old Cecilia Parke married Sir Matthew Ridley of Blagdon in Northumberland in September 1841 she had difficulty at first in exerting her authority over the Blagdon housekeeper, Mrs. Slight. In February 1842, she confessed to her mother that they were 'at daggers drawn about butter', notably about the way it was made. Around six months later she had to use tact in persuading Mrs. Slight to air the bed of a prospective visitor. As Cecilia ruefully admitted, although she 'was a good housekeeper as far as the management of the servants' was concerned, she was 'not particularly so in little *niceties*.'

The high social rank of these landed employers and the strict code of conduct they imposed made it easier for the servants to accept their subordinate status, in most cases. Many were proud to be in 'good service' and felt that working in a country house boosted their social standing. But sometimes a mistress's insistence on the recognition of her superior rank was carried to eccentric lengths. In the late nineteenth century Lady Londesborough, according to her granddaughter, never spoke to any of the staff except for the butler and the housekeeper, while the footmen were 'forbidden to look at each other in her presence'.

Such autocratic behaviour was, however, becoming rare by the Victorian era. More usual was the situation at Blenheim Palace in Oxfordshire, where in the mid-1890s the newly-married Consuelo Spencer-Churchill, Duchess of Marlborough, remembered going round with the housekeeper to check that the correct room allocations had been made for guests attending weekend house parties. Menus had also to be approved in consultation with the chef. The Duchess confessed to feeling sorry for the housekeeper, 'for she had only six housemaids, which was an inadequate staff to keep so colossal a house in order'. A still-room maid was employed, too, to prepare the breakfasts and make cakes and scones for teas, while the French chef presided over a staff of four. There were also five laundresses. The male servants were under the direction of the butler, whose 'chief concern was to keep everyone, including himself, in his place. His rule in the men's department was absolute', declared Consuelo. But without a well-trained and numerous body of servants the large-scale entertaining associated with the Blenheim house parties would have been impossible. High quality servants added lustre to an aristocratic family's reputation for hospitality. It was said that part of Lady Holland's success in high society was attributable to 'the excellence of her chef'. Likewise at Hatfield

House, Lady Salisbury's 'boundless' hospitality was facilitated, according to a daughter-in-law, by the 'lavish splendour in the service, the numbers of menservants, the quantity of food and the abundance of wine and the dessert, with homegrown grapes all the year round and every fruit in season massed in great dishes'. The raising of that fruit was, of course, the responsibility of the gardeners.

Not all landed families could afford the luxury of a housekeeper and in those cases the mistress herself played a more active role in household management. This was true of Mary Ann Dixon of Holton in Lincolnshire, who was widowed in 1871. She not only prepared the household accounts and the shopping lists but oversaw the distribution of stores to the servants, as well as supervising their work and that of the daily helpers. She even cooked from time to time. According to Jessica Gerard, she prepared puddings for dinner parties, 'made pastries for the school feast', and assisted in the processing of the home-killed pig. However, such close involvement in domestic affairs by a mistress was relatively unusual in gentry households. Mrs. Dixon presumably wanted to demonstrate her culinary skills in this way for her own satisfaction, instead of leaving it all to her servants.

However, as Lady Cynthia Asquith pointed out, even when the mistress of a country house did not do any actual housework, she had many other duties and responsibilities to cope with, including the resolution of staff quarrels. 'Domestic politics were... constantly inflamed' wrote Lady Cynthia 'and the necessary intervention a recurrent and preoccupying worry'.

In middle-class homes, especially where one or two servants only were kept, a mistress's direct involvement in the running of her household was customary. Mrs. Panton commended that approach because it provided a good example to the domestics: 'It will not hurt us', she wrote, 'to do a little dusting for once, or even to wash the china.' In farming families, especially in dairying areas, the mistress often worked harder than her maids when making high-quality butter and cheese. In the 1840s the agent of the Marquis of Lansdowne claimed that on Wiltshire dairy farms the wife never allowed a servant 'to manage or clean a cheese, nor to touch it after it [came] out of the vat, thus performing the severest part of the labour herself'. On farms, nonetheless, it was usual for mistresses to expect the maids to help with the feeding of livestock and to go to the fields to assist with haymaking and the corn harvest at the appropriate seasons, alongside their normal domestic duties.

Jane Welsh Carlyle, wife of the famous writer, Thomas Carlyle, was another active participant in the running of her home, During the thirty-two years she lived at Cheyne Row in Chelsea, Jane had thirty-four maids, not counting charwomen, little girls who had 'never been out before' , and other temporary helpers in what was mostly a one-servant household. The fact that they had to sleep in a basement kitchen and that Thomas Carlyle was a finicky employer who, as Jane noted wearily, considered it 'a sin against the Holy Ghost' if a chair or a plate were set 'two inches off the spot they have been used to stand on' , may have partially accounted for the rapid turnover. Each time a new maid was hired she had to learn from her mistress how to make 'Mr. C's sort of soup, and Mr. C's sort of puddings'. But Jane herself, when the mood took her, could be 'a maniac for cleaning – turning out rooms, washing and dyeing curtains, repainting furniture, and insisting upon everything being spotless'. The maid was required to play her part in all this, as well as do the household cooking and washing. Small wonder that one Scottish maid who came in November 1846 left within days, declaring defiantly that 'no woman living could do the work expected of her by the Carlyles'. She was followed in mid–December by an 'Old half dead cook', who also lasted for days only, before the young and cheerful Anne arrived. She stayed for nearly two years, until she left to get married.

In running her household, the mistress's responsibilities included the maintenance of discipline among the staff, and an insistence on good timekeeping. 'Meal times, work times, dressing times, visiting times were at exact intervals', comments Leonore Davidoff, 'and breaches of timekeeping were treated as much a moral lapse as a breach of good taste'. In most homes, servants had to clean the main reception rooms before the family came down to breakfast—something which meant very early rising for them. Lady Cynthia Asquith argued that in 'really well-ordered households it was... the rule that no housemaid should ever be seen broom or duster in hand.'

To achieve this high standard of servant efficiency, experienced mistresses and the authors of household management manuals advocated the drawing up of a list of rules to be observed. Mrs. Haweis, in *The Art of Housekeeping* (1889) suggested it was a good idea to post instructions in the servants' quarters with such reminders as: 'This door to be kept shut'; or 'Please lower the gas if not required;' or 'Breakages not mentioned within the day must be made good.' In large establishments, like Hatfield House, the rules were still more detailed. Staff working there were reminded that bells 'must be answered at once, and Telegrams despatched immediately and delivered on arrival.' There was also a requirement that table linen should be used for no 'other purpose than that for which it [was] intended'. One wonders what nefarious conduct had called forth that particular regulation.

The maintenance of a high standard of hygiene, especially in the kitchen, was rightly regarded as vital for family wellbeing and this, too, was a matter to which mistresses had to give attention. In the main it meant they should visit 'every hole and corner' of the house at frequent intervals, to ensure that windows were opened, dust removed, saucepans kept clean, and drains maintained in good order. These were 'absolute *duties* to be fulfilled, for on perfect cleanliness depends the health of the entire family', declared Ross Murray sternly in *Warne's Model Housekeeper* (1885). That included making sure that food was not left around to encourage mice, black-beetles and cockroaches, all of which infested many dark and damp Victorian kitchens. Mrs. Haweis blamed a lack of vigilance on the part of mistresses for their appearance, declaring that 'no mistress can be considered a fit housekeeper who permits one cockroach in her kitchen'. Bed bugs were another hazard, sometimes being brought into the home with the laundry, where this was sent out. Jane Carlyle had a particular horror of these and in 1849 when she found them in her own 'red bed', a frantic cleaning process was embarked upon. 'All my curtains have been... torn down and sent to the dyers', she wrote; 'not so much to have the colour renewed, as to have the bugs boiled to death.' On another occasion, when Mr. Carlyle's bed was infested, she sent immediately for a carpenter to dismantle it, before embarking on a vigorous cleaning campaign.

Other responsibilities involved keeping a close eye on household expenditure and ensuring that there was no waste. This included the careful preparation of household accounts and the checking of the weight of stores delivered to the house, to make sure that there was no cheating as regards the quantity supplied. Stores needed to be kept under lock and key, and only given to the servants as and when required. Gwen Raverat, the daughter of a Cambridge professor, remembered that even after the cook had been with her mother for almost thirty years, she still 'had to go through the farce of asking for every pot of jam or box of matches to be given out of the store cupboard.' In large households the distribution of stores usually took place at a specific time. At Hatfield House in the 1890s it was 10.30 a.m. on Fridays.

Young and inexperienced housewives often found difficulty in keeping down costs. Louise Creighton, newly-married to an Oxford don, wrote to her mother in January 1872 asking for advice on how to make economical soups, as her own cookery book was of little use: 'all the receipts are fearfully extravagant'. Three years later, when her husband had become vicar of Embleton in Northumberland, she was concerned about the household's food consumption. 'Will you tell me how much butter and how many eggs about you consume a week', she asked her mother anxiously, '... and also your weekly baker's bill? I find it rather hard to make my cook as economical as I should like her to be.'

Even experienced wives like Marion Sambourne in Kensington found it hard to cut waste, especially as cooks regarded it as a rightful perquisite to sell dripping from roasted meat, used tea leaves and similar produce to kitchen waste dealers. Some also demanded that commission be allowed on purchases made for the household and, according to *The Duties of Servants* (1894) they would refuse situations where this was not permitted. Mrs. Sambourne repeatedly complained of 'heavy' books and bills. On 27 January, 1882, she lamented her inability to collect a frock she had ordered from a high-class dressmaker because she could not afford to pay for it at that time: 'Books fearfully heavy'. The next day she received a cheque for £12 5s. from the sale of shares and was then able to visit the dressmaker. But that did not end her worries about household expenditure, for just over a week later on 8 February she complained: 'Books v. high—6¼ lbs of butter & no company in one week. Butcher's book fearfully high'. Part of the problem was that her then cook was not only wasteful but was a heavy drinker. In one fortnight 29 gallons of beer were consumed in what was a household of four maids and a groom. Clearly the cook had been entertaining her friends at the Sambournes' expense. Marion therefore arranged for her to have a pay rise to £25 a year, but '*no* beer'. Perhaps not surprisingly the cook promptly gave notice and for a time after she left, Marion made fewer references to heavy outlays.

With some of the other servants she enjoyed good relations. That was especially true of two of the parlournaids. One, called by her surname of Laurence in Mrs. Sambourne's diary, to distinguish her from the less important housemaid and nurse, worked for the family from the mid-1880s to 1889. Although her main role was to wait at table and open the door to visitors, she helped her mistress with other jobs, occasionally acting as a lady's maid or being sent out to pay small bills and to take the children out. She was more like a companion than a servant. 'Tidied back-yard with Laurence,' Marion wrote in her diary on 7 May, 1885. 'Laurence and self packed all day', was another comment.

It was a convention among the upper classes to act as if the staff attending them were not present, but in small households it was considered important to behave in such a way as to set them a good example.

Gwen Raverat recalled that there were 'many things we might not do, not because they were wrong in themselves, but "because of the maids". We might never sew or knit or play at cards at all on Sunday'. It was part of the same philosophy that family prayers were held morning or evening, and sometimes both, in many homes and that the servants were expected to attend them. The aim was to emphasize the communal nature of the household. Noel Streatfeild, whose grandfather was a clergyman, remembered as a child the 'crackling sound from the maids' aprons as they turned to kneel by their chairs' at the daily prayers in his house. But not all servants seem to have relished these observances. Catharine Paget, the daughter of a leading London medical man, noted drily in her diary that one evening in March 1870, when her parents were away from home, 'The servants without waiting for prayers rushed off to bed before 10!!!' It gave the impression that they were glad to escape a tiresome chore.

Domestic staff probably formed their warmest links with the youngest members of the family. In aristocratic households nurses might have sole charge of the children for weeks at a time while parents were away and, often enough, were expected to escort them on unaccompanied holidays to the seaside or the country. For youngsters whose own parents were too busy or too indifferent to give them love and attention, the servants frequently provided both. Edith Sitwell, whose eccentric baronet father and frivolous socialite mother took little interest in her, found support from her 'dear old nurse Davis' and her father's valet, Henry Moat. His 'friendship with my brothers and me lasted until his death.' Lady Tweedsnuir, too, recalled the 'jokes and laughter' behind the green baize door which marked the servants' quarters and which, from a child's perspective, were 'far preferable to... the drawing-room, where we found it only too easy to knock something over.' Some nurses who had raised a family of children then stayed on in the household, becoming the confidantes of their now adult former charges and perhaps provided with a pension. But close ties were formed with other maids. Anne

Leveson-Gower, Duchess of Sutherland, felt she had 'lost the truest, kindest, and best of friends', when her lady's maid died after forty years' service. And Lady Carnarvon, on a visit to Devon early in 1853, told one of her sons that while she was in Exeter she had 'made choice of 17 Gowns, a Gown for every one of the Servants' at Highclere Castle, the family seat. 'I do not think I shall give them away till Easter, so then you will be there to help me to give them. I have not given them anything for a long time, & I hope they will be pleased with them, for they are all very pretty summer things'.

Not all wives and mothers carried out their duties as mistresses of the household in this exemplary fashion. In the mid-1870s the *Saturday Review* condemned modern women who rose late and then blundered 'in giving orders to the cook'. Such 'slovenliness and carelessness' set 'the servants a wretched example, and afforded [them] endless opportunities for speculation.' Others pursued an active social life to the detriment of their household management responsibilities or, as with Jeannette

Seaton (the former Jeannette Marshall) they took little interest in detailed domestic matters. Although Jeannette was proud of the reception rooms in her new home, she rarely visited the basement kitchen, larders and other offices below stairs. 'The servants— cook, parlourmaid and under-maid were given a free hand'. Such a casual approach would have been condemned by Mrs. Haweis, for whom housekeeping meant 'on the woman's side, much vigilance.' In her eyes, the best housekeeping was 'the largest amount of comfort with the smallest expenditure of cash', and that could only be achieved by a careful mistress.

However, Mrs. Haweis recognized that inexperienced wives could be bullied or cheated by servants who failed to show the expected deferential attitude. 'On the first approach to tyranny, to insolence, to disobedience, to neglect, let the young mistress assert her one solitary power, and dismiss the servant,' she advised. But at a time when a shortage of domestics was beginning to emerge, not all employers were willing to take that drastic step. In the mid-1870s, Louise Creighton at Embleton encountered problems in her household, including with her well-established children's nurse, Eliza. Louise told her mother that Eliza was encouraging the other servants 'to grumble about their food, to go out at all hours without permission, constantly running out herself in the evening without telling me, and being generally moody and noisy in her talk; of course the others take after her. Conversation in the kitchen seems to be far from edifying and Eliza is as bad as the rest'. Initially the Creightons considered dismissing all the maids, but then resolved to give them another chance. 'I mean to draw the reins very tight,' wrote Louise firmly. That seems to have brought about the necessary reform, for less than three weeks later she was cautiously optimistic that things were now running smoothly. Soon, however, the young groom, Rogers, was causing difficulties. Louise described him as 'a troublesome lazy youth', given to telling lies. Eventually he was dismissed. When he left, to the Creightons' annoyance, he went off with his servant's livery, too, But they decided the matter was not worth pursuing, and he was allowed to keep it.

Jane Welsh Carlyle perhaps summarized best the effect of these domestic upsets on many women. 'My goodness,' she wrote to one correspondent, 'why make bits of apologies for writing about the servants—as if "*the servants*" were not a most important—a most fearful item in our female existence!'

CHAPTER 3

Recruiting and Replacing the Servants

During the 1850s and 1860s servant numbers increased with particular speed. Between 1861 and 1871, at a time when the total population of England and Wales rose by 13.2 per cent, that of female servants jumped by just over 25 per cent. In these circumstances the general report of the 1871 census commented sourly: 'Wives and daughters at home do now less work than their predecessors: hence the excessive demand for female servants and the consequent rise in wages.' Although the rate of increase in the number of domestics slackened in the final quarter of the century, the pressure to secure their services did not. Hence the complaints of some mistresses at the end of the Victorian era about their inability to recruit satisfactory maids and the rapidity with which those who were hired moved on to another post, in search of promotion, better pay, more satisfactory working conditions, or merely a more amenable mistress and a change of scenery.

Among male servants numbers had already begun to decline by the middle of the nineteenth century, as alternative job outlets arose to attract them and as middle-class employers preferred the cheaper and more biddable alternative of a parlournaid to the services of a footman or a single-handed man servant. This was less true of the landed classes, for whom an array of liveried male attendants was an important indicator of their social status. At Eaton in Cheshire, the wealthy Duke of Westminster, even in the late nineteenth century, had a retinue of thirty-five indoor servants, plus thirteen laundry maids, forty-one gardeners, fifteen coachmen and grooms, and around two hundred other outdoor staff. Of the thirty-five indoor employees, fourteen were male, including the chef, a kitchen porter, the house steward and eleven valets, footmen, grooms of the chamber and the like, who were under him. Even on a modest estate like Englefield in Berkshire in 1891, the nineteen indoor servants included five men. They were a butler, a valet, an under butler and two footmen. Interestingly none of the Englefield servants had been born in the immediate vicinity of the big house, and the butler and housekeeper were both Scottish. These 'front of house' attendants were expected to have a smart appearance and good stature. According to *The Duties of Servants* (1894), where two or three footmen were kept, employers usually chose tall men of 'equal height to avoid the incongruity of appearance that men servants of unequal height would present'.

Many of the maids in employment were very young, with nearly half of them in the mid-Victorian period aged twenty or less. Only in the final years of the nineteenth century did that change, as young girls became reluctant to accept the restraints of domestic service, preferring to seek jobs in shops, offices and factories. By the 1890's therefore, the bargaining position of mistresses and maids had moved in favour of the latter. According to Charles

Booth in his survey of London during that decade
(when between one in five and one in six of the
nation's domestics worked in the capital):

> A very independent spirit is a marked characteristic
> of the lower classes of servants. Even when seeking
> a place, after arranging with a mistress, they not
> infrequently fail to appear on the specified day.
> They have changed their mind, thinking the work
> too hard, or the neighbourhood too far from their
> friends...

Demand for servants varied from one part of the
country to another, with affluent areas experiencing
the greatest pressure. Thus in 1881, while one in
twenty-two of the total population of England and
Wales was in domestic service, in Bath the proportion
was one in nine of the inhabitants, and in Brighton it
was one in eleven. By contrast, in the mining county
of Durham, a mere one in thirty-one of the people
was a servant.

A large proportion of those taking up domestic

work had been born in country areas and moved to work in towns, where job opportunities were wider. Few employment outlets existed in villages unless a girl was taken on at the local 'big house' as a junior, or could get a post in a clergyman's family or a professional household. Elsewhere they might go to a 'petty place' with a small shopkeeper, artizan or farmer to learn the rudiments of domestic work, but these were usually short-term situations only, from which they would hope to progress to better things or marry. Employers, for their part, preferred country-born staff because they were thought to be harder working, more honest and easier to discipline than their urban counterparts. Occasionally servants were recruited from abroad. For example, French or Swiss lady's maids were hired by the fashion conscious and the affluent, as were French chefs, while Swiss or German nannies were taken on by parents anxious for their offspring to have an early grounding in a foreign language. That applied to Louise Creighton in the late 1870s, when she had a German nanny and a Swiss nursemaid for her children.

For the youngest maids, the move from home and family to employment in a strange household with unfamiliar faces and duties often led to much unhappiness. One former maid, who left her Birmingham home for service in Chiselhurst in October 1888, remembered starting to cry as soon as her father had seen her on to the train at New Street Station. Charles Booth, too, wrote of thirteen-year-old London girls taken by their mothers to their first place in tears. Sometimes they wept 'so bitterly that nothing [remained] but to take [them] home again'. Occasionally parents refused to let their young daughters go to places they thought were too hard but most could not afford to keep them at home once they were old enough to work. For many girls there was little alternative but employment in service once they had reached the age of fourteen or fifteen.

Household manuals stressed the importance of mistresses making clear to staff precisely what their tasks were to be at the time of hiring. At Englefield House, for example, any applicant for the post of butler was told of the scope—and the limitations—of the duties required:

> prayers every morning—punctual—the Plate is under your charge, and you will help clean it. You will lay the Breakfast things, & answer the Drawing Room Bell before 12 o'clock. I keep the Key of my own Cellar, & give you out Wine as it is wanted, of wch. you keep an account. I order everything, and pay for everything—you order nothing except by my direction... You give out the Ale yourself in a fixed allowance [to the other servants]... A Protestant—Healthy—No Apothecaries' Bills [would paid by the employer]—no perquisites... You will valet for me.

Sometimes newspaper advertisements of servant vacancies also indicated what was expected from a successful applicant. Thus on 14 April, 1862, a clergyman from Brighton appealed in *The Times* for three servants. These comprised: 'A good General Servant, must cook well, be strong, active, and an early riser; the other as Housemaid, must be a good needlewoman, and will have to assist in waiting at table; also a smart lad, 15 or 16 years of age, able to clean plate and lamps.' Occasionally other conditions were introduced, such as 'No Irish need apply' or 'Must be Church of England'.

Domestic vacancies could be filled in various ways. For both mistresses and servants, the preferred option was through personal contacts, such as the recommendations of friends and acquaintances or, in the case of employees, by information passed on by relatives or friends already in service. Sixteen-year-old Hannah Cullwick from Shifnal in Shropshire obtained her first post away from her home area in 1849 in a clergyman's household in Lincolnshire. 'My cousin had just left it & they tried me... I learned a good deal from them & I was there 15 months. But I was too young for that place, only the lady kept me on a bit.'

Some country house ladies took an interest in obtaining situations for local villagers. Anne Sturges Bourne frequently wrote to her close friend, Marianne Dyson, for help in placing young maids. In

August 1850, she was seeking a post for her scullery maid, whom she wanted to change: 'she wd. do for that post or under housemaid, also there is a nice little housemaid of John's—only deaf'. In the 1850s she even established a small training school in her own Hampshire home. Her object was 'to substitute good... training for the chance first places [girls] now get'.

Landed families usually had little difficulty in recruiting their staff. Working conditions were normally more comfortable and the food better than in smaller establishments, while there was a stricter demarcation of duties and more companionship from fellow domestics. There was felt to be a greater prestige attached to the work, too. Charles Cooper, who rose from footman to butler, felt he had 'accomplished something when he saw a "well-laid table covered with beautifully kept silver",' and when he was waiting on 'people who matter'. To achieve promotion he had served in several households. For two years he was second footman at Brougham Castle before deciding to leave. He was 'sorry to give up a good place but one had to get on and gain experience'. Although in-house promotions did occur and there were employers like the Yorkes at Erddig near Wrexham who made a practice of it, most servants had to move to a fresh situation if they wished for a senior post. Internal promotions were, in any case, often unpopular with fellow domestics. They resented what Charles Booth called a 'jumped up' servant. In 1837, William Tayler, a single-handed footman employed by a wealthy widow and her daughter in London, commented enviously on the possible promotion of a cousin, compared to his own experience:

> I receved (*sic*) a note from G. Castle to inform me their butler was leaving his place and his master ofered him the place as upper servant and to be out of livery after a bit. George is the luckeyest servant I ever heared of or know. No fellow can have tried to get on more than I have, but I cannot get on so fast as he does... I was four or five years in finding out the way of service, haveing no one to show me, and I taught him

the whole art of service in one year or less.

When personal contacts failed to meet requirements, tradespeople would often act as unofficial recruitment agencies. In Chelsea Jane Welsh Carlyle used the local baker for the purpose, while in July 1868, when Hannah Cullwick was seeking a fresh place in London she was 'lucky enough' to hear of a vacancy from the 'greengrocer's wife'. This was a method recommended by Mrs. Beeton in her *Book of Household Management* (1861). 'ENGAGING DOMESTICS', she declared, 'is one of those duties in which the judgement of the mistress must be keenly exercised...; the plan... to be recommended is, for the mistress to make inquiry amongst her circle of friends and acquaintances, and her tradespeople. The latter generally know those in their neighbourhood, who are wanting situations, and will communicate with them, when a personal interview with some of them will enable the mistress to... suit herself accordingly.'

As literacy standards improved during the second

half of the nineteenth century, advertisements of vacancies or of servants seeking situations appeared increasingly in the national and provincial press. They had the merit of enabling both employers and servants to make a choice over a wide area.

Once suitable candidates had been identified, they could be called for interview. However, this was not without its problems. In 1846, when Jane Welsh Carlyle advertised in *The Times* she complained that as a result she had had a number of 'horrid looking females "inquiring after the place".' Likewise in January 1882, when Marion Sambourne advertised in the *Daily Telegraph* for a cook, she noted that she had interviewed '10 cooks, only 2 at all likely'. Eventually she chose Mrs. Tollman, who arrived on 19 January. Unfortunately her culinary skills proved questionable and she was both extravagant and a heavy drinker. This led to her departure on 8 March. Meanwhile Marion had resumed her search for a fresh cook, and on 2 March went 'about Character of Cook, tolerable'. The new servant arrived six days later. But in January 1883, she was again advertising for a cook, as well as paying 1s. for 'entering Name' at a servant registry office. On 11 January she reported interviewing '2 queer cooks'. The search continued until 12 February, when the new woman arrived.

Sometimes Marion's searches were even more difficult. In 1884 her 'nice cook Fanny' had to leave because she was said to be 'Not strong enough for London'. A hunt for her replacement began early in 1885. Over the period 1 January to 4 February, when a fresh cook came, she interviewed twenty-one applicants. One was rejected because of a bad character reference; eight were dismissed as too old (one being referred to in uncomplimentary terms as an 'old hag') one young cook objected to having to provide a late dinner on Sundays and was therefore unsuitable; one was married and turned out to be pregnant; and one came for interview but announced she was already engaged for a post. Others were rejected without a reason being given. In the interim Mrs. Sambourne employed 'King' on a temporary basis, but found this an expensive option. For less than a month's work King obtained almost £5. This worked out at a rate of about £60 a year, nearly three times the rate Marion usually paid her cooks. She also had to obtain character references from previous employers for likely applicants and usually went in person to seek these. That involved a good deal of travelling around. However, it was an approach recommended by Mrs. Beeton, when she warned against being 'guided by a written [character] from some unknown quarter.'

In the case of country house servants, it was customary for senior staff to appoint their own juniors. Only personal servants, such as a valet or a lady's maid, would be chosen by the employers themselves.

Should personal contacts and advertisements fail to produce suitable candidates, an alternative was to go to a servant registry office. These varied in quality. Some enjoyed a good reputation, but others were thought to be the resort of ill-qualified or immoral staff. Charitable organizations like the Metropolitan Association for Befriending Young Servants and the Girls' Friendly Society also had registries attached to them, as well as lodgings where unemployed domestics could wait until an appropriate vacancy occurred. However, their prime objective was to care for the moral and physical wellbeing of members and to set up clubs or hold tea parties where they could meet their friends. The Metropolitan Association specialized in assisting young former workhouse inmates who had gone to service.

In the 1860s Hannah Cullwick went to one of the 'respectable' registries at the Soho Bazaar in London. There her name was entered in the service book, in company with several other unemployed domestics:

They have prayers there together at a certain hour in the morning, & the man over it all wears a white tie, & speaks to us each about religion & gives us tracts before going up stairs to sit in the room where the ladies come to look at us. So the Soho bazaar is reckon'd a good place to wait for a place at, & I went there for the first time.

I paid ½ a crown [2s. 6d.], the price for the lower servants—it's 5/- for cooks or upper ones. I was shown the way upstairs & where to wait... Then the ladies began to come in, & I felt very nervous till

one lady spoke to me & she ask'd me to follow her,
& that was to another room where the ladies sat &
hir'd you or ask'd you questions after they'd... pick'd
you out...

For those seeking the cheapest maids, applications
were made to workhouses, pauper schools,
orphanages and charities. In these, rudimentary
training was given and inmates were normally
provided with a uniform when they were sent out
to a situation. But often such servants, especially the
youngest of them, were paid very little and became
mere drudges. In 1874 an official report on poor
law girls going to service noted that many of them
went to homes where a few years before wives and
daughters would have done their own housework,
and where family income was too low to permit
them 'to keep a superior servant,' Sometimes, too,
they were despatched to places where the work
was beyond their strength and where their lack of
experience of ordinary family life put them at a great
disadvantage. One mistress complained that when her

young maid first arrived she was not only 'untruthful and pilfered' but she could do little beyond rough scrubbing and laundry work. She knew nothing of cooking and 'could not pare a potato'. As late as 1897 a writer expressed concern at the low wages paid to the youngsters and commended the practice of the Mallow Union in Yorkshire where girls were never sent to a place which paid less than £3 per annum. This sum, he argued, would enable a girl to set money aside in a Post Office Savings Bank account.

Records of youngsters despatched from one poor law establishment, the Central London School District, reveal that fifty-nine girls went to service between July 1888 and December 1889. Most were fourteen or fifteen years of age but two were only thirteen. One of these went to work for a clerk at the Local Government Board, where she was the only servant in a family of eight. The house to which she went had nine rooms and although it was noted that the mistress and a daughter would give assistance, with a washerwoman called in when required, it seems likely that she would be overworked. For this she was paid £6 a year.

Of the fifty-nine girls who went out, fifty-three were in one or two servant households. Their employers varied widely, from clerks, engineers, commercial travellers and shopkeepers to a surgeon, an artist and an author. There were also three 'gentlemen'. In one case, when it was proposed to send a girl to a barrister and his family in Fife, the mother objected and the girl remained in London. Soon after, she went to work for a statistical officer employed by the London County Council, his wife and their seven children. She was to 'help with housework & nursery'. In this instance there were two other servants—a maid-of-all work and a 'lady help', but the house had twelve rooms, and she had to share a bedroom with the other maid.

On occasion the youngsters were ill-treated. In June 1851, Elizabeth Holt, who had been working for a confectioner in the Rochdale area, was returned to Rochdale workhouse after it was reported that she was 'very badly treated and beaten many times a day'. In another case, a youngster first sent out from Rochdale workhouse at the age of twelve in 1855, finally absconded from her post two years later. Over that period she had been sent to four different employers. When she departed she took with her some clothing 'which had but recently been granted her', presumably by the poor law authority.

However, youngsters recruited from workhouses and similar institutions formed a special category of servants. Most domestics moved from post to post of their own volition, or because they were dismissed by their employer for incompetence, insubordination, or dishonesty, or because they were not strong enough for the work. Others left to be married or, in the case of those in large households, because they were bullied by senior staff. Occasionally servants were dismissed because they had become pregnant or for economic reasons. In January 1876, when Louise Creighton's parents were short of cash, she advised them to send away their existing servants 'who have been accustomed to a better state of things' and to keep instead only three maids, 'a cook, a house & parlourmaid combined, & an underservant who should help the housemaid up till one o'clock and the cook afterwards'. She herself supplemented her regular staff during the summer months, when she had visitors, by hiring a 'young girl from the village'. The youngster was then dismissed 'when things resume their ordinary course.' But she received a little training and if she subsequently wanted to take up domestic work, 'I see after getting her a place, and I find this arrangement answers very well. I think it is better to have someone in the house when one is extra busy and not to have continual charwomen'

A few discontented servants, especially among the males, refused to accept insults or bad treatment from their employers. In 1875, Sir Lumley Steward's footman left after being called a 'damned rascal'. Others received orders 'with veiled sulks and insinuations of trouble in the background', or gave deliberately poor service, such as slowness in answering the bell and the noisy banging of doors. In large households staff also had a black list of unpopular establishments. According to one male servant, when news of vacancies in certain houses was received, potential applicants responded, 'Thank you but I don't think I should care to go there.' He claimed to know of two large households which were 'always shunned by servants.'

Occasionally mistresses displayed resentment when favoured members of their staff gave notice to leave. That apparently applied to Anne Sturges Bourne in April 1838, when one of the maids decided to depart: 'I talked to her... She made no complaints & gave no reason but liking to be entirely in London & she was so sulky that I did not choose to say much, tho' I told her my mind abt. her folly... I dare say she does not like being spoken to... I rather hope she may have a harder place & stricter management, as it wd. teach her a good lesson but I shd. be very sorry if she fell into bad hands;' For this reason, servants often preferred to give diplomatic excuses as to why they wished to leave, such as having to nurse a sick mother or being themselves unwell. In this way they maintained good relations with their employer and did not compromise any future character reference.

CHAPTER 4

Life Below Stairs

The duties carried out by servants depended on the position they held and on their age and experience, as well as on the kind of house in which they worked and the attitude and financial resources of their employer. There was an immense difference between the tasks expected of a plain cook in a small establishment, with perhaps one fellow servant, and those in a major household with a large kitchen staff of subordinates to carry out the routine work of preparing ingredients, washing up, cleaning, and cooking the simpler dishes. Albert Gaillard, the French chef at Longleat, home of the Marquis of Bath, had two kitchen maids, a vegetable maid and a scullery maid, as well as a daily woman to assist him during the 1880s. Each morning he wrote out the menus for the day on a slate which he took upstairs for the approval of Lady Bath. But his skills were such that when the family was in London for the Season he was asked to lend a hand at Buckingham Palace if a big dinner party were being held. In return, the Palace chef, who was a friend of his, came to the Marquis of Bath's residence on important occasions to prepare his own specialities.

In 1883, Gaillard was paid £130 a year at a time when the most senior female member of the Longleat staff, the housekeeper, received just £60 per annum. This was despite her responsibilities in superintending the feminine department of the household, as well as distributing the stores to the staff once a week, finding work and repairs for the two sewing maids, and performing 'feats of alchemy' in the still room. There she distilled rose water from roses, produced pot-pourri, preserved fruit, and made jam. As she moved around the house the jangling of the keys she wore at her waist warned juniors of her approach. Housekeepers (and female cooks) were always addressed as 'Mrs.', as a mark of respect, regardless of their marital status.

Even less prestigious chefs, like William Cook, who worked at Englefield House in 1854, earned more than other staff members. In that year he was paid £94 10s. per annum while the housekeeper received £40 a year and the butler, usually regarded as the most senior male servant, received £60. The kitchenmaid was paid £15 a year and the scullery maid £11. The gender difference in pay was made clear by the fact that even in the early 1890s the then female cook was only paid £50 per annum, although the wages of her kitchenmaid had risen to £18 and the scullery maid now received £12 a year.

The largest group of female servants in the Victorian years, however—the maids-of-all-work— were employed not in these prestigious households but in modest homes, where they worked alone or perhaps with one or two fellow domestics. In 1871, general servants comprised nearly two-thirds of the 1.2 million females employed in private domestic service. This may be compared with cooks and housemaids, who contributed less than one-tenth of the total each.

The general servant was expected to carry out a multiplicity of tasks, including cleaning, cooking, running errands and, on occasion, accompanying her mistress when she went out, perhaps to carry her parcels. Mrs. Beeton considered that she was 'perhaps the only one of her class deserving of commiseration; her life is a solitary one, and in some places, her work is never done... [She] has to rise with the lark, for she has to do in her own person all the work which in larger establishments is performed by cook, kitchen-maid and housemaid, and occasionally the part of a footman's duty which consists in carrying messages'. Despite this, she concluded optimistically that a 'bustling and active girl will always find time to do a little needlework for herself, if she lives with consistent and reasonable people'. But if she were not 'quick and active', she would be unable to do that because her duties were 'so multifarious'.

In the late 1860s and early 1870s when Hannah Cullwick was employed as a maid-of-all-work by a widow and her daughters in London, she described some of those duties. She had as fellow servants a house-parlourmaid and a young boy who was not strong enough to carry out the heavier tasks of the household. So Hannah did them instead:

> All the cabs that's wanted I get, & if the young ladies want fetching or taking anywhere I've to walk with them & carry their cloaks or parcels. I clean all the copper scuttles & dig the coals clean the tins & help to clean the silver & do the washing up if I'm wanted, & carry things up as far as the door for dinner. I clean 4 grates & do the fires & clean the [fire] irons, sweep and clean 3 rooms & my attic, the hall & front steps & the flags & area railings & all that in the street. I clean the water closet & privy out & the back yard... I get all the meals down stairs & lay the cloth & wait on the boy & the housemaid as much as they want & if it's my work, like changing their plates & washing their knife & fork.

On occasion she went out on errands or to deliver messages, while 'anything as wants strength or height I am sent for or call'd up to do it.'

The daily round of other categories of servants in small households could be similarly wide-ranging, with cooks expected to help with the cleaning of downstairs rooms, and housemaids combining their cleaning duties and the laborious carrying of cans of hot water to bedrooms for the family to wash, with serving at table and other chores. The detailed timetable prepared by Marion Sambourne for her housemaid in what was normally a three or four-servant household, began at 7 a.m. when she took her mistress's hot drinking water to her room before sweeping and washing the stairs, bathroom and lavatory. She also had to fit in her own breakfast before 8 a.m., when she carried up the hot water for her mistress's bath. After this, she drew the blinds, emptied the bath, removed it, and continued with other duties. By 8.30 a.m. she was starting to clean the drawing room, while her mistress had breakfast in bed, taken to her by the parlourmaid. Bedmaking followed, with detailed instructions given on the cleaning of the bedrooms. The wardrobes, for example, had to be 'dusted *inside* and out'. Between 1 p.m. and 1.20 p.m. the housemaid had to be ready to answer the hall doorbell so that the parlourmaid could put on a fresh uniform in readiness for serving luncheon. After this, hot water had to be taken to her mistress's bedroom so that she could wash her hands before eating. The maids had their own dinner at 2 p.m. and when this was over the housemaid's detailed tasks continued, with each activity carefully timed. Thus between 5 p.m. and 6 p.m. she had to look over Mrs. Sambourne's belongings 'and take any things needing mending'—a chore she likewise had to perform. At 8 p.m. the family dined and she had to help with the serving, before again going to the bedrooms to turn down the beds, clean the washstands and make sure that the chamber pots were ready for use. Supper for the servants was at 9 p.m. and at 10 p.m. she took letters to the post before she finally went to bed—having worked a fifteen-hour day, with five short breaks for meals. On Mrs. Sambourne's weekly 'at home' day, when she received her friends, the work included not merely giving the drawing room a 'special' clean but arranging the flowers, emptying the aquarium, and putting the tea table ready: 'all silver taken down on tray'.

Despite this formidable programme, and a similarly detailed one for the parlourmaid, the girls found opportunities to gossip and giggle in the kitchen. Marion often commented on this and wished they might be quieter and better behaved. At least once, in February 1885, she dismissed the cook and the housemaid for gossiping, though it is not clear if this was because they were talking about the family. Too great a display of curiosity about an employer's correspondence, conversations or callers was always resented by the employer. Indeed, Jane Welsh Carlyle was advised by a friend to dismiss immediately a maid who had apparently looked at her letters, since this would soon lead 'prying into all your comings and goings'.

The multiplicity of duties expected of female servants in small households applied to single-handed men servants, too. They were required to act as a valet to male members of the family, to trim the lamps, clean the candlesticks, serve the meals, take messages, and go out with the carriage. This was true of William Tayler, who was employed by Mrs. Prinsep and her daughter in London. However, his diary for 1837 also reveals that, unlike the women servants in such households, he had freedom to go out, for example to pay bills on the family's behalf. Sometimes this led to his receiving a modest commission from the shopkeeper. He obtained occasional tips from visitors to the house, too, and estimated that in total these 'perquisites' yielded about £10 or £15 a year, to supplement his basic pay of £42 per annum.

William's diary shows he had a fair amount of spare time, which he spent in reading, sketching and painting. He and his three fellow female servants often entertained their friends in the kitchen or went to celebrations in other households. 'I went to a party today', William wrote on 27 December. 'It was gave by some servants. There was card playing, fiddleing and danceing and some singing, plenty to eat and drink'. He paid clandestine visits to his wife and family, who were lodged not far away, too. The existence of his wife was kept secret because married servants frequently found difficulty in getting places. Employers feared they might pilfer food or other goods to help support their family, or perhaps their loyalty to their employer would be less than absolute.

As part of his ceremonial role, William went out with the carriage when his mistress and her daughter paid calls or attended special functions. At these times he was sometimes entertained in the servants' hall by the staff of the house they were visiting, and enjoyed gossip and refreshments, including copious supplies of alcohol. However, on 19 May, when the daughter went in the carriage she stayed out longer than he 'thought she aught to of done, therefore I gave her a little row for it. I hope it will do her good. I served the old lady the same way the other day and it did her a deal of good.' It is unlikely that in grander establishments such impertinence would have been tolerated. William remained with the Prinseps until his mistress's death in 1850. He then moved to another household.

The conditions and the relative informality which existed in these small properties differed greatly from those in the homes of the social elite. There the staff were extremely rank conscious and jealously protected their position in the servant hierarchy. This particularly struck the Frenchman, Hippolyte Taine, when he visited England in the 1860s. 'Each has his post rigorously defined,' wrote Taine. 'The work is divided, no one either trespasses on, or trusts to another.' He compared the upper servants to 'a species of sergeants, who ... do their work conscientiously, with perfect punctuality and regularity, at the appointed time'.

At the head of these households on the male side was the house steward or the butler, while the housekeeper was the most senior female servant. Valets and ladies' maids had a special position because of their sartorial skills and intimate relationship with their employer. This sometimes made them objects of suspicion among junior members of staff, who suspected them of tale bearing. If there were no valet, the butler or a footman might fill that role for male members of the family and their guests, while the housekeeper or the housemaids took on a similar responsibility for the females.

The specialization of functions applicable to housemaids was recalled by Margaret Thomas when she worked in a large country house in Yorkshire. There 'the fourth housemaid worked entirely for the staff, the third for the schoolroom,... and helped the second, who had to be downstairs at 4 a.m. every morning to get the sitting-room done before breakfast. The second housemaid had a medal room to keep clean where the medals were set out in steel cases, and had to be polished with emery paper every day... The head housemaid did light jobs'.

Butlers did not wear livery and their duties included care of the plate chest and the wine cellar. They also overlooked the arrangement of the table for each meal, before waiting at it. They were expected to exercise strict control over their subordinates, particularly the footmen, For as one servant handbook advised, 'under servants are never ... comfortable, much less happy, under lax management'. At Longleat, according to Lady Bath, the 'butler was far too grand a figure to roll up his sleeves and work in his own pantry; and in the dining room he would serve only the wine and the more imposing dishes.' The under servants, by contrast, 'were kept strictly in their place and had little liberty'.

Footmen were chosen for their good looks and height. They combined a ceremonial role with various menial duties, like polishing boots, looking after the lamps, cleaning the silver and laying the table, under the direction of the butler or under butler. They played their ceremonial part when, dressed in elaborate livery and, in some households, with their hair powdered, they waited at table, answered the drawing room bell, sounded a gong before dinner, and went out with the carriage or with messages. They were hired partly as symbols of the family's wealth and importance and their earnings were influenced by their appearance. Hippolyte Taine claimed that 'the ornamental look [was] worth to them as much as an extra £20 a year', although he also added sourly that their 'stuck-up airs have become proverbial'. In great houses they spent much time changing their clothes and standing idle in the front hall ready to open the door to callers.

The discipline imposed by senior servants and the training they gave their subordinates were rigorous and even harsh. As Jessica Gerard notes; 'Having to combine instruction with operating the department [which they controlled] created pressure to teach recruits quickly, and this sometimes degenerated into bullying.' 'We lower servants had to walk the chalk-line,' declared one male domestic. 'Obey, or else'. Some young servants left because of this, but most accepted it stoically as part of the learning process. Margaret Thomas, for example, worked as a kitchenmaid in London for a very clever cook. Although the woman was rather bad-tempered, no doubt because of the hot, badly ventilated kitchen in which she worked and the need to produce high quality dishes each day, Margaret 'ignored all the hard things she said to me ... because I admired her skill'.

The distinctions drawn between members of staff as regards the duties they performed and their status within the household also applied to the serving of their meals. In small establishments the servants ate in the kitchen, but in large households the senior servants would eat in the steward's or the housekeeper's room, while their juniors ate in the servants' hall or, in the case of kitchen workers, in the kitchen itself. The main exception was the mid-day dinner in the servants' hall. Then, as at Longleat and many other similar properties, the under servants would troop in and remain standing at their places until the senior staff had filed in. These entered in order of domestic ranking and after the first course had been served, they would depart in a similar fashion, headed by the steward's room footman, who at Longleat carried out the joint with great ceremony. The seniors retired to the steward's room for the rest of their meal, while the housemaids and sewing maids at Longleat hurried off with platefuls of pudding to eat in their own sitting room. In most grand households, however, the juniors remained behind in the servants' hail and would be free to gossip with one another while they finished the meal. When the seniors were present they had to remain silent. This seems to have been common practice in many large houses.

Because both male and female staff were employed in these major establishments, great care was taken to segregate them when they were at work, and to keep their sleeping quarters well apart. The maids often slept in the attic although at Blenheim Palace they apparently lived 'up in a tower where there was no running water', much as housemaids there 'had... lived for nearly two centuries', according to the Duchess of Marlborough. The menfolk frequently slept in the basement or in a special wing. At Erddig, the Yorkes required their footman to sleep with his bed in front of the only door to the safe where the silver was stored, for security reasons. But in-house flirtations did take place, as ways were found to 'dodge the housekeeper's eagle eye'.

In small households, too, there were usually strict rules prohibiting 'followers'. However, some mistresses took a more liberal stance. Louise Creighton was quite happy that two of the maids had 'young men' in the village. The men were not yet in a position to marry and she thought this would encourage the servants to stay in their posts.

Occasionally, despite the restrictions, clandestine meetings in large households had unfortunate consequences. At Calke Abbey in Derbyshire, Sir George Crewe commented drily on the pregnancies of two maids. One involved his footman, Samuel Williams, and his wife's lady's maid; the other, his mother's coachman and her lady's maid. At Hesleyside in Northumberland, the Charltons kept on their butler, Inkley, for a number of years, despite his notorious womanising. They did so because it was so difficult 'to get a sober and efficient butler in such a house for drink as Hesleyside.' Eventually, though, his conduct caused a severe breach with the long-serving housekeeper and he was dismissed.

In all servant-keeping households the restrictions on the dress and conduct of staff and on their opportunities for contact with the outside world gave rise to tensions and quarrels 'below stairs'. Margaret Thomas, employed at a large Yorkshire property, complained that there was 'no mateyness in that house, everyone seemed too conscious of their position... We, in the kitchen, found our friends among the outside staff.' The housemaids favoured the footmen but members of the kitchen staff, like Margaret, disliked them because 'they used to stand silently criticising us, tapping out a tattoo on the table if we weren't ready with the meals'.

Yet there could be happy times in these large houses, too. At Erddig, the maids all went to one room at bedtime to gossip with one another, while at Eden Hall, Charles Cooper recalled there were 'eighteen servants kept, so we had plenty of fun.' Sometimes recreational facilities were supplied for the staff by their employers. Taine mentioned places where there was a library provided for them as well as various board games for them to play. Elsewhere sporting facilities were offered and cricket matches arranged for the menfolk. At Longleat and certain other houses, servants' dances were organised. These were attended by the outside servants as well — the unmarried grooms and gardeners. 'I like to think of those still room maids and housemaids discarding their printed chintz dresses and muslin caps for their evening finery, prinking in front of their mirrors before going down to the hall to dance', wrote Lady Bath, years later. The housekeeper, though, kept a close watch on the younger maids, 'reprimanding the over-frivolous.'

Some senior servants found satisfaction in their work. A skilled cook enjoyed producing gourmet meals and a butler took pride in a well-laid table. Head gardeners cultivated high quality vegetables and flowers, and won prizes at exhibitions. Even in small households, staff could develop a proprietorial attitude. At Alderley Edge, Katharine Chorley remembered that the gardener 'ruled the garden like a grand vizier ... I dared not pick a flower or eat a strawberry without permission'. He even resented her parents donating fruit and flowers to their friends and to Manchester hospitals.

The amount of time off which servants were allowed depended on the attitude of the employer. Although it was customary by the end of the period for servants to have half a day a week free, plus some time on Sunday, and a week or a fortnight's holiday annually, that by no means applied everywhere.

William Lanceley, who worked in a number of large country houses, noted that staff were usually offered a holiday once a year, normally when the family was away. But according to him, few took up the offer. His first holiday in four years' service 'was three days, quite enough at that time,' for servants found 'cottage homes and food were no comparison' to living in a mansion.

In small households the situation was still more variable. Marion Sambourne's maids seem to have had time off at irregular intervals, and they might have to postpone an outing if there were company. This happened to Laurence, the parlourmaid, early in April 1886, when Marion recorded that the maid had gone out a week later than planned 'on acct. of company'. Mrs. Layton, employed as a general servant at Kentish Town in London during the 1870s, recalled spending much of her spare time reading 'trashy novels', some borrowed from the maid next door. She was allowed out on Sundays only, from 3 p.m. to 5 p.m. one week and from 6.30 p.m. to 9 p.m. the next. She spent the free hours going for a walk, but then her mistress asked her to take the children of the family with her as well. As she had them during the week, she felt this was a great imposition and the two parted.

It was in these circumstances that indoor domestic service became increasingly unpopular, especially among the young. That was not so true of outdoor posts, such as gardeners, grooms and gamekeepers. Their numbers continued to rise sharply to the end of the Victorian era. By contrast in the second half of the nineteenth century, male indoor servants in private households declined from just over 74,000 in 1851 to less than 48,000 by 1901.

Although the number of females in service did continue to rise, in the final decades of the century it was among older age groups that the increase occurred. In 1881 43 per cent of female servants had been under twenty; by 1901 that had fallen to less than 35 per cent of the almost 1.3 million still engaged in private households. With improved educational opportunities and a rise in alternative employment outlets, youngsters, both male and female, were reluctant to accept the restrictions of servant life and to adopt the deferential attitude expected by their employers. The uniform or livery they wore depersonalized them and the fact that they were often treated as if they were invisible when going about their duties underlined their social inferiority. Even those, like Mrs. J. E. Panton, who ostensibly sympathized with them, could nonetheless display wounding insensitivity. In *From Kitchen to Garret* (1888), she exhorted her fellow servant-keepers to 'make real friends of those who live under our roof', but then commented that although she would like 'to give each maid a really pretty room' that was impossible.

No sooner is the room put nice than something happens to destroy its beauty; and I really believe servants only feel happy if their rooms are allowed in some measure to resemble the homes of their youth, and to be merely places where they lie down to sleep as heavily as they can.

She also advised against allowing them to keep their boxes in their rooms, for 'they cannot refrain somehow from hoarding all sorts of rubbish in them.'

By the 1890s mistresses were lamenting the 'independence' of young maids and their readiness to move to a new place. An official survey of domestic staff in London during the middle of that decade revealed that 47 per cent of the general servants covered, 33 per cent of the cooks and 35 per cent of the housemaids had been in their current post for less than a year. Only 5 per cent of the general servants, 9 per cent of the cooks and 6 per cent of housemaids had stayed with the same mistress for ten years or more.

Some employers reacted to the situation by cutting back on resident workers and recruiting daily cleaners instead. In the case of landed families, falling rental incomes gave an added economic impetus to the reduction in numbers, or perhaps led to the replacement of expensive indoor men servants by parlourmaids.

Technological innovation played a part, too. The introduction of the telephone reduced the need to send footmen out with messages, while piped hot water to bathrooms and electric lighting to replace oil lamps and candles, were other labour-saving devices. On a minor scale, the use of carpet sweepers eased the work of housemaids. Commercial enterprises played a role as well. Many landowners closed their personal laundries and used the services of outside businesses. The Duke of Bedford patronised two firms of dyers and cleaners for Woburn Abbey at the beginning of the twentieth century, while a local baker supplied bread to the household at around the same time. Other products like jams, pickles, chutneys, cordials and polishes were purchased from retailers rather than being produced in a still room.

Domestic service remained the major employer of female labour up to the First World War and, indeed, beyond. Even when Gwen Raverat married in the early twentieth century she admitted it would never have occurred to her 'that I could possibly be the cook myself, or that I could care for my baby alone, though we were not at all well off at that time. It was not that I was too proud to work ... it was simply that I had not the faintest idea how to begin to run a house by myself.' But by 1900 growing numbers of mistresses were coming to recognize that this automatic dependence on servants to ensure the efficient running of their home was already under threat. In the twentieth century life 'below stairs' was never to be so unquestioningly accepted by the populace at large as it had been in its Victorian heyday.